# I'm Still in His Hands

# I'm Still in His Hands

*The righteous falls seven times, and get back up.*

*"My Father, which gave [them] to me, is greater than all; and no [man] is able to pluck [them] out of my Father's hand."* – John 10:29

Douglas L. Ross

 All scripture quotations are taken from the King James Version of the Bible. Words are replaced in some scripture quotations with more contemporary words for emphasis and clarity.

In chapter eight of this book, permit me to use the term *overcomer.* The word is not found in the dictionary as one word. The word *overcome* is found, and is defined as *to win or be successful, especially in spite of obstacles.* My use of the term *overcomer* is to describe a person with these attributes.



ISBN: 978-0-9796077-1-4
ISBN: 0-9796077-1-X

Printed in the United States of America.

Library of Congress Number: 2007905039

# *Dedication*

I hereby dedicate this book to Pastor Harold Wilson, and the members of Victory Life Fellowship. To Bishop Gerald Glenn, and the members of New Deliverance. To Greenbrier Baptist Church where I began my pastorate. To Dr. Michael Freeman of Spirit of Faith Christian Center, to Dr. Frederick Price of Crenshaw Christian Center—*thank you for allowing us to be a part of FICWFM, we value the fellowship.* To Dr. Don Turner, Dr. John Taylor, and the faculty of International Bible College. To all the members of God Chasers International Church, whom I pastor, you are the best. God is going to take you higher. Your set time has come.

A special thanks to Viola Scott, my dear, sweet mother—I love you. To my *father* Robert, my sister Dottie, my brother Charlie, my son Chriss, Rashad, all of my nieces and nephews, cousins, my father-in-law Jerry Gaiters, and all of my in-laws.

*Last,* but not least, a very special dedication and thanks to my wife Gwen. I thank you, honey, for the poems you contributed to this book and the contributions you've made towards my years of joy and happiness. I love and cherish you as my wife and friend.

# Contents

# *FOREWORD*

It is not very often that one has the opportunity to read material that truly reflects what the Word describes about the grace of God. I am pleased to announce that Pastor Douglas Ross takes a very comprehensive look at the love, grace, and mercy of God in his book—*I am Still in His Hands.*

There is much misunderstanding about certain areas of God's Word when it comes to sinning and falling short of God's glory. We sometimes make mistakes and blow it in life. This book however breathes life, hope and encouragement that will inspire any believer to go on in their walk with God, without being hindered by past mistakes. Reflecting upon my experience with television, and interviews; when mistakes are made the words "take one, take two, take three" are used frequently. A mistake is a MIS-TAKE. When one has made a MIS-TAKE, it's encouraging to know that "take one, two, three, and even four is available to you through the grace of God.

The information presented in this book allows one to know that with Christ you are granted another "take" in life. I highly recommend this book to anyone who is interested in the truth. *I am Still in His Hands* is a wise investment into one's spiritual growth and development.

*– Dr. Michael Freeman*
*Senior Pastor*
*Spirit of Faith Christian Center – Brandywine, Maryland*

# *Introduction*

When our children act out and misbehave, we, as parents, discipline them. Though they may be naughty and troublesome at times, they are still our children. The same is true when it comes to our relationship with God our Father. When we sin, God will discipline us. God is not pleased with our sinning, but he never abandons us; he remains our Father. The Bible says that those who the Lord loves, he disciplines (Hebrew 12:6).

I wrote this book with you in mind. If you are a Christian struggling in your walk, the devil will try to bring condemnation upon you and cause you to question or doubt your salvation. Other Christians may even look down on you because of your challenges. I want to encourage you to press forward in the Lord. If you've fallen in your Christian walk, get back up and press forward.

This book begins with a short story about a man who loved the Lord, but made some bad choices, and eventually fell into condemnation and despair. I see this happening often in the Body of Christ. We must understand that God is our keeper, and he loves us so much that he sent his son to die for our sins. God says he is married to the backslider. God wants us to understand that even though there may be problems in the relationship, he's still our Father.

As you read this book, remember that it is our duty to present ourselves as living sacrifices, holy and acceptable unto God. The Bible says this is our reasonable service. This book does not make light of sin. When we sin and live in a way that's not pleasing to God, he grieves. I write this book for you, praying that you will never fall short of pleasing God. I pray that you never sin, but if you do, I want you to know that you have an advocate with the Father; his name is Jesus (1 John 2:1).

## Short Story:
## The Devil's Deception

# CHAPTER 1

"As the clay [is] in the potter's hand, so [are] ye in mine hand." – Jeremiah 18:6

It was a cold winter day. The worship service at Holiness Cathedral Church was long, but the word preached this particular morning was provoking and filled with inspiration. Theodore Whitesmith had been a member of the church for two years. He loved the church, and his church family loved him.

Two years earlier, Theodore received Christ as his Lord and Savior, and through his conversion, he was delivered from drugs and alcohol. Since receiving Christ, Theodore had enjoyed a near picture-perfect life as a Christian. As a member of the helps ministry and an usher, Theodore attended church on a regular basis and never missed a service. He remained faithful in his tithing and regularly gave to those in need. Everyone liked him. The pastor of Holiness Cathedral was in prayer about ordaining Theodore into the diaconate.

This particular winter morning found Theodore joyful and optimistic. Today was the day he would pop the question to Jessica. Jessica was a member of Holiness Cathedral. She grew up in the church and served on many of the auxiliaries. Theodore and Jessica had become close friends, and for over a year now, they've been fellowshipping outside of church functions and become very dear to one another. Jessica had influenced Theodore to join the church after he began attending two years ago. She witnessed to him coming out of a whiskey store one Saturday morning. That day, Theodore received Jesus into his life and was given an invitation to visit Holiness Cathedral.

"God is good," Theodore thought to himself. "Just two years ago I was drinking and drugging, and now I have a future. As soon as Jessica says yes to my marriage proposal, I'll be on my way to having a lovely wife. Yes, God is good."

Dreams of marrying Jessica had dominated Theodore's mind since the day she met him coming out of the whiskey store. Today would be a day of rejoicing. Things were looking up for him. A new job, new car, money in the bank, his ministry at the church, everything had fallen into place. The only thing needed now was Jessica as his wife.

Jessica hadn't attended church service this particular morning. Her job was doing their yearly inventory, and she was required to work. She went in at eight that morning, but it was only a four-hour shift, so Theodore concluded she would be home by the time he arrived at her house.

The drive took about twenty minutes. She lived on the outskirts of the county, off Rock Mountain Road, in a subdivision called Washington Farms. Upon arriving at her house, Theodore noticed that the door was up on Jessica's garage. It was strange, because Jessica was particular about closing her garage door. "Well," he thought, "maybe she just forgot to close it today."

Theodore pulled into the driveway and parked behind Jessica's car. He walked to her door and rang the doorbell.

"Who is it?" a voice asked.

"Theodore," he replied.

The door opened, as if by magic, and standing in the doorway was Jessica. They smiled, greeted each other, and Jessica invited Theodore in. "This is a surprise," Jessica said with a bright smile.

Theodore smiled back and said, "I needed to talk with you."

It was the moment of truth. Excitement and fear seem to engulf Theodore at the same time. He was excited about the prospect of her saying yes to his proposal, and fearful of her saying no. Each emotion struggled for dominance.

"Well, take a seat," Jessica responded. They sat on the living room couch. "What's on your mind?" Jessica asked.

Theodore paused for a moment and nervously began. "Jessica, we have been friends for nearly two years now. I feel closer to you than to anyone else. "I think—" He paused. "I would like for us to become even closer. Jessica, what I'm trying to say is—would you marry me?" There was a moment of silence. It was as if the world had come to a halt, become mute, and awaited Jessica's voice. Jessica stood, walked towards the window, and stared into the yard.

"I don't know what to say," she whispered.

"Just say yes," Theodore replied. Once again, the room fell into a deep silence. The minutes that passed seem like hours, and then there was a break in the silence.

Jessica turned, looked at Theodore, and apologetic-cally said, "I'm sorry, but I can't. I feel close to you, and I truly enjoy your company, but I can't marry you. I see you as a brother, and I enjoy that relationship with you. I'm sorry, but I can't."

Silence returned to the room. Theodore rose from the couch, stared at the floor, and said, "I must admit I'm disappointed, but I respect your answer. I'll find my way out." He walked towards the door and left the house. Hurt and bewildered, he got into his car. The drive to his house was lonely and plagued with thoughts. He thought to himself, "This isn't the way it's supposed to happen."

Three weeks later, early Sunday morning, as Theodore prepared for church he received a phone call from one of his old girlfriends. It was Nancy. He hadn't talked with her in almost three years. "Hey, Nancy," Theodore exclaimed in surprise. "This is a surprise. What's going on?"

Nancy replied, "I was thinking about you and decided to give you a call. I thought it would be nice if we could maybe get together and talk about old times."

Surprised by the call, Theodore replied, "Sure, let's do that." They made plans for lunch that week, and after a fifteen-minute conversation, Theodore resumed getting ready for church. He arrived at church about fifteen minutes late. It was his first time being late for church since joining. Theodore loved the Lord and his church, but for the past couple of weeks, his mind had been elsewhere. He hadn't completely recovered from Jessica's rejection.

As time passed, Theodore and Nancy's relationship rekindled. They began to see more and more of each other. One night, after dinner at Nancy's house, the couple began to talk about their past. Their past involvement had been a very physical and passionate relationship. The conversation eventually led to an embrace. They began kissing passionately; Nancy got up from the couch with Theodore's hand in hers and led him into the bedroom. Nancy wasn't a Christian, and *that* night Theodore forgot that he was a Christian. They had sex, and Theodore spent the night.

The next morning, after leaving Nancy's house, Theodore returned home, but things were different for some reason. He wasn't himself. "Maybe it's because I haven't prayed this morning," he thought. He kneeled in the living room to pray, but could think of nothing to say to the Lord. Theodore thought about Nancy and last night. "God is not pleased with what I've done," he grieved. "I can't pray because God has left me," he painfully concluded.

Feelings of guilt overtook Theodore, and he began to weep, bitterly and uncontrollably. It seemed as though hours had passed, but the tears continued to flow. He thought about Jessica. She would be so discussed with him if she ever discovered what he had done. "How could I be so weak? God can never use me now," he thought to himself.

Weeks went by. Theodore's attendance at church became very erratic, and then he stopped attending altogether. Theodore's prayer life ceased to exist. He felt God didn't want to hear anything he had to say. The pastor and many of the brothers from the church called him, trying to encourage him to come back to church, but to no avail. Theodore and Nancy began to see more and more of each other. Nancy loved to have a good time. She often had friends over for drinks and party treats.

One night at Nancy's house, Theodore decided to have a beer. He hadn't touched alcohol in over two years. "It wouldn't hurt to have just one beer," he said to himself. After drinking the beer, he kissed Nancy and went home.

The next morning, while preparing to go to work, Theodore felt a sudden need to call his pastor. He picked up the phone and began to dial, then canceled the call. "He doesn't want to hear from me," he concluded. Theodore felt that he'd lost his salvation and everyone in church would look down on him. "After I've gotten myself together I can call the pastor and go back to church," he reasoned.

Theodore started drinking. It began with a beer every now and then, but soon he began to drink rum and coke. At first, it was just on weekends, but it soon became a daily thing. His job performance and attendance began to suffer. One day, after a night of heavy drinking, Theodore arrived at his job two hours late. He had already been warned about his increasingly poor attendance and tardiness. He rushed to get to his workstation, but before he could take his position on the line, his supervisor stopped him.

"Come to my office," he motioned to Theodore. After entering the office, the supervisor said bluntly, "Theodore, I'm sorry, but I'm going to have to let you go. Your attendance and performance no longer meets the requirements and expectations we have of our employees. I'm sorry."

Flabbergasted, Theodore walked out of the office, left the warehouse, and drove home. Sitting at his kitchen table, he poured rum and coke into a glass and began to sip the drink. "God is still mad at me," he thought. I've lost my ministry, my salvation, Jessica, and now my job—what's next?" He pondered in his mind, "what's next?"

Theodore sat at his kitchen table for hours, drinking. The *half of gallon bottle* of rum was now empty. "Nancy! I'll go to Nancy's house," he decided.

He struggled to his feet, picked up his keys, and staggered out of the house to his car. It had begun to rain. While driving down the wet pavement of Boulevard Street, a thought suddenly became clear to Theodore. "I know how to straighten out the mess I've made of my life. I've disappointed Jessica, I've disappointed the pastor, God is disappointed with me, and my salvation is lost. There's only one thing left for me to do. Yes, that's it," he decided.

Theodore made a u-turn and drove back towards Rock Mountain Rd. Jessica lived off Rock Mountain Road, a mountainous road on the outskirts of town that extended into the mountainous region of the county. Driving up the mountain, Theodore thought about the church. He wished he could return, but he felt he could never go back after what he had done. "My presence would only bring shame to the church and congregation," he thought. "They know I've lost my salvation, and I am no longer a Christian; no, I can't go back there." He continued to drive.

Reaching the highest point on Rock Mountain Road, Theodore turned the wheel sharply to the right and drove his late-model car through the railing. The car plunged violently down the side of the mountain. A vision appeared to Theodore. Jesus was weeping and holding his hands out to him. He glanced to the right and saw his pastor and church family praying and calling his name. He focused his eyes to an image to his left and saw the devil laughing uncontrollably, Theodore suddenly realized the devil was laughing at him. Visions of family members and love ones flashed across Theodore's eyes. Just before the car struck the rocks at the bottom of the mountain, Theodore cried out, "Jesus, forgive me for not being able to keep my salvation! I'm sorry." Then he heard a voice whisper, "Nothing and no one can snatch you out of my hands. For by grace are ye saved through faith; and that not of yourselves: [it is] the gift of God."

The car slammed into the bottom of the mountain and exploded into flames. The aftermath could be seen for miles. As the car burned, Theodore's cell phone echoed from the smoke and wreckage. It was Jessica on the other end, calling to tell Theodore that she'd changed her mind, and if he still wanted to marry her, she would be delighted to be his wife.

# CHAPTER 2

The story you've just read is fictional. The characters and the places are imaginary, but the story is similar to many real life situations. Imagine the agony of feeling you've lost your salvation and God has turned away from you. Imagine the torment of thinking that your church family is looking down on you because of a bad choice you've made. Can a person lose their salvation once God grants them eternal life? That is the question I want to address. There are so many different views on the security of salvation that it could leave many confused and uncertain of the truth. It is God's desire that we know, without a doubt, the truth. I want to show you what God's word has to say about this subject. Scripture tells us we should study to show ourselves approved, a workman who need not be ashamed, rightly dividing the word of truth. I ask you to pay close attention as we deal with this important issue.

Let's walk through the word of God and search for answers to this very important question concerning salvation. Proverbs 3:5-6 tells us:

"Trust in the LORD with all your heart; and lean not unto your own understanding. In all your ways acknowledge him, and he shall direct your paths."

***Before we proceed, let's humble ourselves before our Heavenly Father in prayer:***

Dear God and Heavenly Father,

You are our Father, and we are your children.

I come before you, as humble as I know how, asking for your guidance.

I ask for your anointing. I do not pray only for myself, but for all who will read this book.

Open our minds as we search for truth, and let our hearts be settled on your word.

Father, help me to teach your unadulterated word as you give me the ability to write this book.

Father, you said we are saved by grace; help us to fully understand what this means.

You said that if a man lacks wisdom to ask you, and you will give it to him liberally.

Father, give me wisdom concerning this subject, that all who read this book will have the full understanding of salvation.

Thank you Father for your mercy, your grace, and your kindness.

It is you we love and worship, and no one can take your place.

*In Jesus' name, I pray*—**Amen!**

We must allow God's word to be the judge of all matters concerning life and our eternal destiny. Jesus Christ is the author and finisher of our faith. He wrote the book. He's the one to turn to with our questions. When in doubt, ask God; and let God be the judge.

My sister Bea loved the Lord and his house. She suffered from sickle-cell anemia, and endured much pain because of it. In pain, she would often press her way to God's house. She felt that if she could just get to God's house, everything would be okay. She would arrive at church in pain, but leave pain-free. My sister Bea often had questions concerning the security of salvation. She went to be with the Lord a few years ago, and I know without a doubt that she's at home with him. A few days after her passing, God spoke to me while driving west on Interstate 295. He told me she was safe in his arms. I was relieved. Her moments of uncertainty caused unnecessary grief in her life. It is not God's desire that we live in fear of losing our salvation. God has not given us a spirit of fear, but of love, power, and a sound mind. We *must* come to a place of certainty concerning our eternal destiny.

Just because you have fallen short of God's glory, that is no reason to throw in the towel. Pay close attention to the counsel God has given me; it could save you from much guilt. *Sin does not end salvation.* If you have fallen into sin after giving your life to the Lord, repent. Get back up and continue to run the race. I do not advocate living a riotous life. God forbid that we intentionally and habitually commit sin. These things I write to you, that you sin not, and to let you know that if any man sin, we have an advocate with the Father, his name is Jesus (1 John 2:1).

### *I Just Don't Feel Righteous*

"For if we sin willfully after we have received the knowledge of the truth, there remains no more sacrifice for sins, but a certain fearful looking for of judgment and fiery indignation, which shall devour the adversaries." – Heb. 10:26 - 27

One of my brothers in Christ (I will not mention his true name), but for the sake of sharing this story, I'll call him Mitchell. Mitchell was, and still is a true brother in Christ, and a very dear friend to me. It wasn't long after I started our local congregation in Richmond, Virginia, that Mitchell began coming by the church. He was distressed about his salvation. Mitchell talked about how God was no longer pleased with him and how God had stripped him of his salvation. Mitchell had committed a sin. The fall bothered Mitchell so much that it robbed him of his peace and joy. Many Christians believe salvation can be lost, and they live in fear of this daily.

Fear of losing one's salvation torments believers and causes guilt, fear, and condemnation to be rooted in their hearts. What a predicament. Opponents of secure salvation often refer to Hebrew 10:26-27 to support their view that salvation is something we must hold on to by staying good and sinning not. This verse creates a problem in the minds of many Christians. Certainly, our belief in any subject should be supported by the word of God, but we need to make certain that we are correctly interpreting the scripture and not reading into it what we want it to say.

It is easy to twist scripture, but keep in mind that we are told to rightly divide the word of truth. We must read out of the scripture what God has put there, and not what we want it to say. We must *exegete* and not *eisegete* scripture. *Exegete* means to study a text and interpret it according to what's in the text, whereas *eisegete* means to "*read into*" scripture something that really isn't there. If we are to rightly divide the word, we must abide by the rule of *exegeting* the scriptures.

To clarify the issue of salvation's security, we will keep the above mentioned rule in place. Now, remember what the scripture says in Hebrew 10:26-27.

"If we sin willfully, there remains no more sacrifice for sin."

Mitchell felt that because he had committed a sin, *and according to Hebrew 10:26-27*, he'd lost his salvation. But look closely. This verse actually refers to a person who has yet to receive salvation. He discovers that Christ is Lord, and then refuses to accept him as Lord and Savior. *Let's paraphrase the verse*:

"For if we sin willfully (*rejecting Jesus*) after we have received the knowledge of who he is, there remains no more sacrifice for sins, because there's no one else who can forgive you of your sins."

There is no more sacrifice for sin, because Jesus Christ is the only way to eternal life. He died once for our sins, and he will not come back and sacrifice himself again. The willful sinning mentioned in this verse is a rejection of Christ after finding out who he is. This verse does not refer to a person who is already saved. Mitchell was not condemned by this verse; if he were, we would all be in trouble, because it says that if you willfully commit a sin, there's no more sacrifice available for you. Thank God that our Father says we can come boldly to his throne of grace.

The story in chapter one depicts the tragic results of a person feeling guilty about bad choices they've made. The ending is a warning of how far guilt can take a person. Becoming a Christian doesn't mean we will suddenly live righteously. Some believers are able to walk away from certain behaviors immediately after conversion, while others go through a process of change. God does not look at the righteousness of our good deeds. He looks at the righteousness of Christ in us. Once we become believers, Christ enters and abides in us, and we become the righteousness of Jesus Christ.

"And being found in him, not having mine own righteousness, which is of the law, but that which is through the faith of Christ, the righteousness which is of God by faith." – Phil. 3:9

Christ did it all. We can do nothing. No matter how good we are, we fall short of the glory of God. Salvation came to us by our receiving Jesus. Salvation is kept, not by our righteousness, but by having Jesus in our lives. We are declared righteous because of the righteousness that is found in him. Believing and receiving is the only thing God requires of us for salvation. God gives us salvation, and the Holy Spirit secures it until the day of Christ's return.

We may fall and make mistakes, but the righteous falls seven times and gets back up. If you've fallen in sin, get up, and get back into the race. You can run this Christian race, so get up from your pity party and run for the Lord.

Salvation, the Gift for Life

# CHAPTER 3

"In whom you also [trusted], after that you heard the word of truth, the gospel of your salvation: in whom also after that you believed, you were sealed with that Holy Spirit of promise." – Eph. 1:13

Faith comes by hearing, and hearing by the word of God. The apostle James wrote, "of his own will he begot us with the word of truth." The apostle Paul stated that the gospel is the power of God unto salvation for all who believe. There is saving power in the gospel. We must first understand the power of God's word and the necessity of believing it. Believing God's word releases the power of his word into our lives.

Our faith in God is authenticated by our belief in what God has said. Every Christian's attitude should be, "*If God said it, then it is so.*" We must never waver from this position; our faith depends on it. "Let us draw near to God with a true heart in full assurance of faith, having our hearts sprinkled from an evil conscience, and our bodies washed with pure water."

We must come to God with confidence and full assurance, without wavering, doubting, or confusion. The word of truth is the word of God, and faith demands we live by every word that proceeds out of the mouth of God. We often make the mistake of picking and choosing which word, or scripture we desire to embrace. When we do this, we place ourselves outside God's perfect will and violate the scripture that encourages us to live by faith. We *must* acknowledge that *all* of God's word is true, and every man is a liar.

**Power to be His Child**

We all like to be and feel secure. True security starts with us knowing our condition and eternal destiny. As Christians, our condition is saved, and our destiny is to forever be with Jesus. Before we can understand salvation, we must first understand how we became a child of God in the first place. We didn't become Christians because of our good deeds and right living. We became children of God by faith. We asked, and received Christ into our lives.

"But as many as received him, God gave them power to become his sons, [even] to all that believes in his name." – John 1:12

To all who received him! All who received Jesus into their lives are granted the power to become children of God. Everyone who receives him, who accepts that Jesus is Lord and Savior, all who have confessed with their mouths and believed in their hearts that God raised Jesus from the dead, shall be saved. We received power to become God's sons. The word "power" in this verse comes from the Greek word *exousia,* meaning "power, authority, right, liberty, power of choice, and physical and mental power." When we come to Jesus and receive him, God gives us the right and privilege of becoming his child. I know you've heard it said we are all children of God. Unfortunately, this isn't true. Only to those who have received Jesus does God give the power to become his children. To have a relationship with God, to be called his child, you have to accept Jesus into your life. Jesus said, "I am the way, the truth, and the life; no man cometh unto the Father, but by me." To get to the Father, you have to come through the Son, there's no other way. You can't get to him by way of any other religion. You can't get to God the Father as a result of your good looks, and you can't get to him through your own good deeds and merits. Jesus is the only way. "For God so loved the world that he gave his only begotten son, that whosoever believes in him should not perish, but have everlasting life." We read in 1 John 5:12, "Whosoever shall confess that Jesus is the Son of God, God dwells in him, and he in God." God dwells in all who confess that Jesus is the Son of God. In 1 John 5:12, we read, "He that has the Son hath life; [and] he that have not the Son of God have not life." If you have Jesus in your life, you have life. It is something you already have, not something you work for, but something you have. If you have Jesus, you have life! It is *Zoe*, meaning, "of the absolute fullness of life, both essential and moral, which is of God." Being alive in God's presence is Zoe—a life active, vigorous, devoted to God, and blessed in this world and the world to come. Zoe is having eternal life. Salvation and eternal life begins the day you accept Jesus as your Lord and Savior. Eternal life comes from God, and it is kept safe and secured by the Holy Spirit. That's good news to my ears. Excuse me; I need to give him praise.

"Thank you, Jesus! Hallelujah, glory to your name!"

**The Way to Salvation - *Continues***

Let's continue the thought and deal with how you came to receive salvation in the first place. Understand, we keep our salvation the same way we received it. The way to receive salvation is found in the book of Romans. *Pay close attention.*

"But what says it? The word is near you, [even] in your mouth, and in your heart: that is, the word of faith, which we preach. That if you shall confess with your mouth the Lord Jesus, and shall believe in your heart that God has raised him from the dead, you shall be saved. For with the heart, man believes unto righteousness; and with the mouth, confession is made unto salvation. For the scripture says, whosoever believes in him shall not be ashamed. For whosoever shall call upon the name of the Lord shall be saved." – Rom. 10:9-11 (13)

Salvation is granted by grace to everyone who accepts Jesus into his or her life. As the scripture says in Romans, if we confess with our mouth and believe with our hearts that Jesus died for us and was raised from the dead, we shall be saved. Also, it concludes that whosoever shall call upon the name of the Lord shall be saved. This is called salvation by grace. We did nothing to earn it; it is granted because we asked Jesus to come into our lives. No devil in hell, or on earth can take salvation away from us! The world didn't give it, and the world can't take it away—*you know the song.*

If I don't keep all ten of the commandments, will

God take salvation away from me? Can I lose my salvation? *You may be asking this question.* As I've just stated, no devil in hell or on earth can take salvation from you, and God is not an *Indian giver*. The term "*Indian giver*" is used to describe someone who gave you something and later took it back. God is not like that; the gifts and calling of God are without repentance, and so is your salvation. Your salvation is secure.

**You Are Sealed until the Day of Redemption**

"And grieve not the Holy Spirit of God, whereby you are sealed unto the day of redemption." – Eph. 4:30

When God grants salvation, he does not intend to take it back; he provides a safety net to keep you from losing it. The Holy Spirit seals you until the day of redemption. To place a seal upon a thing is to secure it. Our salvation is secured by the sealing of the Holy Spirit. No one can break the seal. No one can tamper with it. The protector makes certain that the seal of salvation remains affixed until Jesus comes for his possessions. All Christians belong to Jesus; we were all bought with a price. Jesus paid our debt with the shedding of his blood.

The Bible warns us not to grieve the Holy Spirit. The Holy Spirit is our helper, our comforter, our constant companion—and he is our sealer. His care and labor for us is performed with joy and gladness. But we grieve the Holy Spirit when we lie, walk in anger, gossip, speak evil, and walk in fear.

There are other ways to grieve the Holy Spirit. *The third person of the Trinity*, the Holy Spirit is God. Because God is holy, it is his desire that we be holy also.

In the list of the behaviors given as grievous to the Holy Spirit, I want to highlight "evil speaking." Evil speaking comes from a Greek word, *blasphemia,* meaning blasphemy—sacrilegious and reproachful speech injurious to divine majesty. After Jesus' death on the cross, the shedding of his blood for the remission of our sins, and his proclamation that it was finished, for anyone to suggest that more is needed for salvation, or that we need a degree of works to keep it, is blasphemy (*evil speaking*). Jesus said it was finished—no more is needed.

When you suggest that you can lose your salvation, you are saying that what Jesus did on Calvary wasn't sufficient to keep you saved. Jesus' death on the cross provided all we needed to receive salvation by the grace of God. To think that we have to maintain a performance of good works to hold on to our salvation depreciates Jesus' death, and abates what his death means in relation to our eternal destiny. To think such a thing would be grieving to the Holy Spirit and an insult to the Lamb that was slain for the sins of the world. Jesus did it all, and he said it was finished. Once saved, always saved! Now—I've said it, and I will not take it back. **Your salvation is secure.**

Impossible To Be Renewed

# CHAPTER 4

"For [it is] impossible for those who were once enlightened, and have tasted of the heavenly gift, and were made partakers of the Holy Ghost, and have tasted the good word of God, and the powers of the world to come. If they shall fall away, to renew them again unto repentance; seeing they crucify to themselves the Son of God afresh, and put [him] to an open shame. But, beloved, we are persuaded better things for you, and things that accompany salvation, though we speak in this way." – Heb 6:4-6

Opponents of secure salvation refer to Hebrew 6:4-6 to support their case that a person can lose his salvation. Keep in mind that we must not read into the word or twist it to make it say what we want it to mean. The danger of this is the risk of coming away with the wrong meaning, leading to error and misled faith. Mitchell was misled and thought he was no longer saved because of a sin he committed. His works became his foundation in the security of his salvation. My friends, you can't do anything to save yourselves, and you can't do anything to keep yourselves saved. Securing your salvation is a task for the Holy Spirit. *Consider this*:

"For [it is] impossible for those who were once enlightened, and have tasted of the heavenly gift, and were made partakers of the Holy Ghost, and have tasted the good word of God, and the powers of the world to come, If they shall fall away, to renew them again unto repentance."

It says it is *"impossible"* to renew a person that has fallen away from Christ to repentance. The phrase *"tasted of the heavenly gift"* is talking about a person who hears the word and accepts Jesus as their Lord. If an individual accepts Christ, has truly been granted salvation, and falls away from the faith and rejects Christ, it is *impossible* to renew him or her, or bring that person back to salvation. In a situation such as this, Christ would have to be crucified all over again. What are you saying, Pastor? I'm saying that if a person loses his or her salvation, it would be impossible to renew them because Jesus would have to be crucified all over again. Jesus died once for the sins of the world; he will not be crucified again. Notice the word *"if"* in this verse. The key is found in the word *"if."* If a person fell away from the faith or lost their salvation, it would be impossible to renew, but then Paul says:

"But beloved, we are persuaded of better things for you, and things that accompany salvation, though we speak in this manner." – Heb. 6:9

In the previous verse, Paul is speaking hypothetically, not literally. He doesn't believe it is possible for a Christian to fall away from or lose their salvation. But *if* it were possible for a true believer to fall away, Paul explains the result of such actions. The Bible speaks literally and figuratively. The Bible also speaks in parables, and here Paul speaks hypothetically. In rightly dividing the word of truth, we have to understand the mind-set of the writer. *Let's observe the verse closely:*

"But, beloved, we are persuaded better things of you, and things that accompany salvation, though we speak in this manner." – Hebrew 6:9

Or to paraphrase, "Even though I say these things, I really don't believe this can, or will happen to those who are saved."

We, as Christians, are sealed and kept by the Holy Spirit until the day of Christ's return. Our salvation is signed and sealed as we wait for the day of redemption. God wants us to know without a doubt that we are safe and secure. *"Put you on the helmet of salvation."* That helmet protects you from doubt and fear of losing your salvation. My friends, we are saved by grace! It is a gift of God.

Do we continue in sin because we are saved by grace? God forbid! To prove our love for God, we must endeavor to keep his commandments.

## IT IS BY GRACE, BY GRACE!

"For by grace are you saved through faith, and not of yourselves: [it is] the gift of God: Not by works, lest any man should boast." – Eph 2:8-9

There are parts of Eph. 2:8-9 that many people don't

understand. To allow God to open our understanding of this verse, let's break down each section. "For by grace are we saved through faith." The verse clearly reads that we are saved by grace through faith. Grace is God's unmerited favor. We did nothing, can do nothing, and will do nothing to earn it. It's a gift from God. It comes from his agape (*unconditional*) love for us. When we confess our belief, and receive Jesus as our Lord and Savior, God grants us salvation in accordance with his grace.

"It is not of yourselves: [it is] the gift of God."

This tells us that our salvation is not of ourselves; it's nothing we have done. Not by our own efforts. We could never be good enough to achieve salvation. We all have fallen short of his glory. We can't work for salvation. Our works aren't good enough. You can't buy it; there's not enough money in this world, and there's no other method to acquire it. God knew the dilemma we were in, so out of his love, he placed us under the dispensation of his grace. Salvation is a gift from God! It is a precious gift—the ultimate gift. Whosoever calls upon the Lord shall be saved. You called on him, and God saved you. God did it, and you can't undo it.

You May Not Be Perfect

# CHAPTER
# 5

"Arise, and go down to the potter's house, and there I will cause you to hear my words." - Jer. 18:2

In the eighteenth chapter of the book of Jeremiah we find a perfect example of our secured salvation in God. Jeremiah is told to go to the potter's house; God would cause him to hear his word there.

"Then I went down to the potter's house, and behold, he wrought a work on the wheels." - Jer. 18:3

The Bible tells us that Jeremiah went down to the potter's house, just as God had instructed. When God instructs us to do something, our trust in him should cause us to respond in obedience to his word. We will never receive from God unless our faith is directed by what God says. When Jeremiah arrived at the potter's house, he observed the potter working on the wheel used for clay. The potter was diligently perfecting his creation. Jeremiah said the potter fashioned a work on the wheel. The potter knew what he was doing and performed his work with skill and precision.

A potter's wheel is a revolving horizontal disk, on

which clay is shaped manually into vessels. To operate it, the potter kicks or propels the disk *or* (crank) to keep the turntable spinning. This spinning enables the potter to easily fashion the clay as the potter desires. The psalmist said of God, "Thy hands have made me and fashioned me." Just as the potter fashions the clay, God fashions us. The Bible tells us we are fearfully and wonderfully made, and marvelous are the works of God.

"And the vessel that he made of clay was marred in the hand of the potter." – Jer. 18:4

Jeremiah looked closely at the vessel the potter was fashioning and noticed that the vessel was marred (*flawed or damaged*). It is not stated that the potter did anything in error, *or* how the imperfection in the vessel came to be, but we know that the vessel was marred. Imperfections in the clay could certainly have rendered the vessel flawed. Likewise, when we come to Christ, we may come with flaws that render our Christian walk imperfect. Though we are flawed and have problems in our lives, God doesn't give up on us. The vessel was marred, but the potter didn't give up on the vessel; neither did he cast it out. Just because you might have issues you need deliverance from, God will not cast you out.

"So he made it again another vessel, as it seemed good to the potter to make [it]." – Jer. 18:4b

The potter believed the vessel, *though marred,* was usable, and he decided to make it again. Would the potter repair the vessel, or would it be an entirely new one? Notice the phrase "make *it* again." The potter was going to make *it* again. The word "*it*" signifies the same vessel. He was going to take the same vessel and make or create it again. The new vessel would be the same vessel, *but not the same vessel.* The Bible tells us that if any man is in Christ, he is a new creation. Old things have passed away, and all things have become new. We are just like the vessel that was made again. We may appear to be the same individual, but we aren't the same. As the potter was able to make the vessel again, God is able to make all things new in your life.

Before we can experience the fullness of what we have become in Christ, we must first allow God to do a work in our lives. We must be still and allow God to shape and mold us. The clay is submissive to the potter's hands. Likewise, we must place ourselves in the hands of God and be submissive to his will. We may have problems to deal with, but God hasn't given up on us. Don't allow the devil to make you feel God can't use you. We must be confident of this very thing—that God, which hath begun a good work in us, will perform [it] until the day of Jesus Christ (Phil.1:6). God made us, and he can fix what ever needs fixing in our lives. God will perfect that which concerns you.

"So he made it again another vessel, as seemed good to the potter to make it."

The potter remade the vessel, as it seemed good to him. The potter creates the vessel to fulfill a specific purpose. If the purpose of the vessel is to hold water, a cracked vessel could not perform the task. It would seem good to the potter that his vessel be completed without any flaws that would hinder the fulfillment of the vessel's purpose. Likewise, God has a plan for our lives. It seems good to God, *our Father*, that we be transformed into the image of Jesus Christ, to fulfill the purpose he has for our lives. To become what God desires of us takes submission to his will. The clay becomes what the potter desires because it is submitted to the potter. The clay doesn't move in the hands of the potter, but allows the potter to shape and mold it as the potter desires. Likewise, we must be still and allow God to shape and mold us. We must submit to God's will and become what God desires us to be.

As we meditate on the story of the potter and the clay, we must not overlook the most important aspect of the text. When Jeremiah came into the potter's house, he saw the potter hard at work. The vessel wasn't perfect, and the potter had to make it again. The potter was skillful in his ability and made the vessel new. But there is one aspect of this story that we don't want to overlook.

"Behold, as the clay [is] in the potter's hand, so [are] ye in mine hand." – Jer. 18:6

Even though the vessel was marred, even though the vessel wasn't perfect, *I need you to understand* – it never left the potter's hands. The potter didn't throw the vessel away because it was marred. Likewise, though you might have problems, have fallen short of God's glory, and may not be where you should be in your Christian walk—even with all your issues—you're still in God's hands. You haven't been discarded. God will never leave or forsake you. My friend Mitchell didn't understand that all he had to do was confess his sins to God. If we confess our sins, God is faithful and just to forgive us of [our] sins, and cleanse us from all unrighteousness (1 John 1:9). Your salvation is secure. No matter what shape you are in, as the potter made the vessel again, God can fix the flaws in your life. You're still in his hands.

We don't lose our salvation because we take a fall in our Christian walk. If we fall, we get up and press toward the high calling of God. God loves us. He wouldn't abandon us because we made mistakes. God said he was married to the backslider. I repeat, the righteous fall seven times, and they get back up. If you fall, get back up. Stay in church, keep praying, God can fix it.

God Sees You Different

# CHAPTER 6

"But the fearful, and unbelieving, and the abominable, and murderers, and whoremongers, and sorcerers, and idolaters, and all liars, shall have their part in the lake that burns with fire and brimstone: which is the second death." – Rev. 21:8

"For without [are] dogs, and sorcerers, and whoremongers, and murderers, and idolaters, and whosoever loves and makes a lie." – Rev. 22:15

"Nor thieves, nor covetous, nor drunkards, nor revilers, nor extortionists, shall inherit the kingdom of God." – 1 Cor. 6:10

A great number of people will not be able to partake of the gift of salvation with Christ, but you're not one of them. Rest assured, if you have received Jesus as your Lord and Savior, you are saved, and you will inherit the kingdom of God. The individuals described in the above verses will have no place in the kingdom because of their refusal to repent and allow Jesus into their lives.

Second Corinthians 5:17 reveals that all who are in Christ are new creatures, or "*new creations*." We cease being the person we used to be; God sees us differently. Many of us were bound by one, *or* more of the sins mention in the above verses; we were sinners, but God sees us differently now. God sees Christ in you; he sees the person you were created to be. God separated our sins as far as the East is from the West, and he said our sins he will remember no more. We must trust God to keep us walking according to the nature of the person we were created to be. If at times we fall short of representing that new person, we must get up, repent, and continue the walk.

**Tempted in all Points, yet without Sin**

"For Christ [is] the end of the law for righteousness to every one that believeth." - Rom. 10:4

The word *"end,"* mentioned in this verse, comes from the Greek word, *telos,* meaning, "the limit at which a thing ceases to be, that by which a thing is finished, the end to which all things relate, the aim, and purpose." To put it literally, the word *"end"* is the fulfillment *or* completion. Jesus is the fulfillment of the law to everyone that has received him. The Jews sought to keep the law in order to attain righteousness, but no one through works could ever attain the righteousness of God; all have fallen short. Adam, Noah, Abraham, Samuel, David, Elijah, Daniel, and John the Baptist, *to name a few*, all fell short of the glory of God. Then came Jesus, the only begotten of the Father, full of grace and truth.

Jesus walked among us and was tempted as we are, but was without sin. You might ask how could Jesus have been tempted by adultery *or* divorce when he was never married? How could he be tempted to highjack a plane when there were no planes in that day? The Bible never said Jesus was tempted to commit every sinful act that man has committed; the scripture says he was tempted in all points, as we are. We must understand the difference. Three points of temptation stand at the root of every sinful act man has ever committed. The devil has no new tricks; he uses the same points of temptation to tempt you today that he used to tempt Jesus two thousand years ago—the same points of temptation that he tempted Eve with in the garden.

*First John 2:16 tells us,* "For all that [is] in the world, the lust of the flesh, and the lust of the eyes, and the pride of life, is not of the Father, but is of the world." Clearly, in this verse, we find revelation of the three points *or* areas of temptation that are in the world. The *first* area mentioned is the lust of the flesh; *second,* the lust of the eyes; and *third,* the pride of life. From these points of temptation, spring all sinful acts. The lust of the flesh causes married men to commit adultery, single men to commit fornication, and rapists to commit rape. Lust of the eyes causes men to covet their neighbors' goods, *to* never be content with the things that they have. The lust of King David's eyes enticed him to desire Bathsheba. Lust of the flesh caused Eve to partake of the forbidden fruit. *"And when the woman saw that the tree [was] good for food..."* (Genesis 3:6). Eve saw the tree, and her flesh wanted the fruit thereon. The devil also tempted her with the lust of the eyes. *"She saw that the tree [was] pleasant to the eyes"* (Genesis 3:6b). And to put the icing on the cake, the devil tempted her with the pride of life. *"A tree to be desired to make one wise*" (Genesis 3:6c). The pride of life could cause sins ranging from not being submissive to authority, *to* racism, *to* easily being offended. Individuals have even committed murder because of pride provoked anger.

Jesus was tempted in all three points. He was first tempted with the lust of the flesh. The devil said unto him, "If thou be the Son of God, command this stone that it be made bread" (Luke 4:3). The devil knew Jesus hadn't eaten in forty days, and he tempted him to eat.

The devil tempted Jesus with lust of the eyes. "And the devil, taking him up into a high mountain, and showed him all the kingdoms of the world in a moment of time. And the devil said unto him, "All this power will I give thee, and the glory of them, if you would therefore worship me" (Luke 4:6-8).

The devil's final temptation was the pride of life. "And he brought him to Jerusalem, set him on a pinnacle of the temple, and said unto him, "If you are the Son of God, cast thyself down from hence: For it is written, he shall give his angels charge over you, to keep you. And in [their] hands they shall bear you up, lest at any time you dash your foot against a stone" (Luke 4:9-11). The devil tempted Jesus to prove that he was the Son of God and that God cared for his safety. Don't allow the devil to entice you to prove God's love for you. Pride causes men to think they have to prove themselves.

The Bible says that Jesus was tempted in all points, yet did not commit one sinful act. First Corinthians 10:13 informs us that, "no new temptation has tempted you but such as is common to man." Consider what this means. Men weren't tempted to commit credit card fraud in biblical times, but we see it today. Children weren't tempted to carry guns to school and shoot their teachers and classmates in biblical times, but we see it today. The temptation that caused men to steal wheat and grain two thousand years ago is the same temptation that causes men to commit credit card fraud today. Because of technology, access to information, and cultural behavior patterns, we have new ways of committing sins, but the point of temptation is the same—lust of the flesh, lust of the eyes, and pride of life.

The good news is this—Jesus (though tempted in all three points) did not sin; he fulfilled the law of God. The law had to be fulfilled before mankind could be redeemed. God needed someone who could redeem his people, so Jesus stepped down from the throne of heaven to get the job done. No other man could do it. Even today, we could never fulfill the law by our own merits and good deeds. All have fallen short of the glory of God. None are righteous, not one. You can be a goody two shoes, a righteous Rudy, or a Mother T, but you will still fall short of the glory of God.

"For Christ is the end of the law for righteousness."

Since we have established that Christ fulfilled the law, the second half of this verse is very important; Christ was the fulfillment of the law for a reason. We find in the second half of this verse the reason and result of his fulfilling the law. "For righteousness to everyone that believes." Christ fulfilled the law for (the) righteousness of all believers. We couldn't do it on our own, but Jesus made it possible for us to be declared righteous. He fulfilled the law for our justification. We are the righteous in Christ Jesus, and we were given this gift by faith (Romans 5:17).

"For therein is the righteousness of God revealed from faith to faith: as it is written, the just shall live by faith. Even the righteousness of God [which is] by faith in Jesus Christ unto all and upon all them that believe: for there is no difference: Being justified freely by his grace through the redemption that is in Christ Jesus." – Rom. 1:17 - Rom. 3:22, 24

The righteousness of God is made known or available to us by faith. Righteousness is made available in all areas of our lives—in our walk, our talk—doing it God's way comes by faith. We all have faith in one thing or another, but I'm speaking of faith in Jesus Christ—faith in the work he did on Calvary. We must have faith that we are justified through the grace afforded us through believing in Jesus. We are freely justified by his grace, that we may live our lives by faith in him. Many of us find it hard to believe that Jesus completed our salvation and healing on the cross, but he did. Jesus did it all, and the work was perfect. No longer, *as Old Testament saints had to do*, would man have to bring a sacrifice for sin year after year!

"Christ being in you, the body is dead because of sin, but the Spirit is life because of righteousness. For they, being ignorant of God's righteousness and going about to establish their own righteousness, have not submitted themselves unto the righteousness of God." – Rom. 10:3

*In review*—the Jews tried to attain the righteousness of God by keeping the law, but no one can keep the law in its entirety. One must keep every letter of the law. To be found righteous by your own good deeds and character, you must be perfect. No sinful act, no sinful thoughts—your heart must be cleansed of all ill feelings towards your neighbors. Your eyes must always be focused on the right things, twenty-four hours a day, seven days a week, three hundred sixty-five days a year; all the days of your life, you have to remain perfect, sinless, and holy. It can't be done. Only by the grace of God can you be found righteous and acceptable. God sees Jesus in us, and because of Jesus, God considers us righteous. Thank God for Jesus!

How to Know You Are Saved

# CHAPTER 7

"He that has the Son has life; [and] he that has not the Son of God has not life. These things have I written unto you that believe on the name of the Son of God; that ye may know that you have eternal life, and that you may believe on the name of the Son of God." – 1 John 5:12-13

You can know that you have eternal life (*salvation*) and that your salvation is secured. God wants us to be at peace, knowing the status of our eternal destiny. The scripture says, "If you have Jesus in your life, you have eternal life." That's it. Believe on the name of the Son of God, and you shall not perish with the unsaved, but shall have eternal life. The Word is final. *According to 1 John 5:13*, these things were written that you may know without a doubt that you have eternal life, *if* you believe in Jesus and have him *in* your life. I don't know about you, but as for me, men can talk and sound as convincing as they would like, but I'm going to believe the report of the Lord. Saved by grace, not by works.

Does this mean we continue in sin? **No, God forbids!**

Are you in need of further proof concerning the security of your salvation? Do you need a witness? I encourage you to listen to your spirit and not your mind (*flesh*).

The Spirit itself bears witness with our spirit, that we are the children of God. – Rom. 8:16

## Such Were Some of You

"For it had been better for them not to have known the way of righteousness, than, after they have known [it], to turn from the holy commandment delivered unto them. For if after they have escaped the pollutions of the world through the knowledge of the Lord and Savior Jesus Christ, they are again entangled therein, and overcome, their latter end is worse with them than the beginning." – 2 Pet. 2:20-21

"Nor thieves, nor covetous, nor drunkards, nor revilers, nor extortionists, shall inherit the kingdom of God." – 1 Cor. 6:10

God's word is true! We can't take away from it, or attempt to add to it, but we must rightly understand it. I wish to enlighten you to the fact that God will never leave you or forsake you; your salvation is secured by grace. The Bible contains scriptures that may *seem* to contradict that statement. I believe in facing obstacles that stand in the way. Take a closer look at the scriptures, and you will find that there are no contradictions in God's word.

Many of us are set in our ways. We heard something said, and we adopted it into our belief without verifying it.

*I repeat*—some people belief in salvation has its foundation on a *naughty or nice philosophy*. They believe, if we are good, we will remain saved, but if we're bad, we will lose our salvation. If you apply the *naughty or nice philosophy* to the keeping of your salvation, you remove yourself from the grace of God. We must believe God and his word. We must not frustrate the grace of God by vainly trying to keep ourselves saved. I know I'm being repetitious, but I want to drive this home, *we are saved by grace, and not by works; it is the gift of God!*

Allow me to submit this to you—God is still on the throne and his word stands, regardless of what we believe; that's why it is so important that we understand what God says. *First Corinthian 6:10* is clear—"No thieves, nor covetous, nor drunkards, nor revilers, nor extortionists shall inherit the kingdom of God." Paul was talking to the church at Corinth. They were having many problems. The Corinthians were fighting each other as well as experiencing problems in the church. Many of the same problems are found in churches today. Paul wrote to the church and conveyed the truth concerning thieves, the covetous, drunkards, revilers, and extortionists. But then he says in the next verse, "such were some of you." We need to underline and highlight this—***"and such were some of you."*** Celebrate, because these labels no longer fit who you are. A first grade English student knows that the word "*were*" is past denotative and means that what we *were* before becoming Christians is in the past. If you were a thief, drunkard, or extortionist, it's all in the past, God sees you different now; God sees Christ in you.

As Paul conveyed this revelation to the church at

Corinth, we must embrace this truth today. The good report is ours. Old things have passed away, and all things are new. We are no longer what, and who we use to be.

"And such were some of you: but you are washed, but you are sanctified, but you are justified in the name of the Lord Jesus, and by the Spirit of our God." – 1 Cor. 6:11

When we accepted Christ as our Lord and Savior, something happened to us. We were washed in his blood—that purifying blood that washes away all sins. We were sanctified and set apart from the world and condemnation of it. We were justified and declared righteous in the sight of God. It was all done, not by works, but by the power of the name God has place above all other names—the name Jesus—and the Holy Spirit sealed the deal. It was a done deal when you gave your life to Jesus. All the details pertaining to our salvation were taken care of. God had it planned before Adam and Eve sinned; even before the foundation of the world, God had a plan to redeem us.

"For it had been better for them not to have known the way of righteousness, than, after they have known [it], to turn from the holy commandment delivered unto them.

For if after they have escaped the pollutions of the world through the knowledge of the Lord and Savior Jesus Christ, they are again entangled therein, and overcome, the latter end is worse with them than the beginning.

But it is happened unto them according to the true proverb, the dog [is] turned to his own vomit again; and the sow that was washed to her wallowing in the mire." – 2 Pet. 2:20-22

## You're not a dog, or a pig

Keep in mind that such *were* some of you, but not anymore. In the epistle written by Peter, he talks about someone who had come to the knowledge of Jesus Christ. This knowledge of the Lord Jesus Christ was not a spiritual knowledge, but a *notional* knowledge. A spiritual knowledge of Jesus Christ evokes relationship with him. *Notional* knowledge only generates ideas. "For it had been better for them not to have known the way of righteousness." The individuals that Peter describes were never regenerated; they were still considered dogs. They were in church, but the church wasn't in them. They simply came into some knowledge of Jesus, and through that knowledge, they sought what they considered a better way of living. They believed attending church would bring them good luck and change their situation. They never truly became Christians. They had a form of godliness, but denied his power (2 Timothy 3:5). They heard the word preached Sunday after Sunday. They heard the testimonies of the true believers and witnessed God move in the lives of his people. Things even improved in their own lives. They looked like Christians, but they never totally surrendered to Jesus; instead of embracing the Lord, they eventually turned from the way of righteousness. They rejected the truth, the holy commandments of God, *and* instead of surrendering to

Christ, they drifted back into the world. Now, the proverb comes true—a dog turns to his vomit again, and the pig that was washed has wallowed in the mud.

The sad fact is, these *churchgoers* were still compared to dogs and pigs. They were never new creatures in Christ, for had they been new creations, they would not have been called dogs and pigs. You can wash a pig, put perfume and nice clothing on him, but as soon as he gets an opportunity, a pig will return to and wallow in mud. *Such were some of you,* as Paul emphasized in his writing. We are now washed in the blood of Jesus. We wear robes of righteousness, for we are unto God a sweet fragrance of Christ (2 Corinthians 2:15). We are a royal priesthood, a holy nation; old things have passed away, and all things are made new. No longer are we compared to dogs, or pigs, or drunkards, but we are now called saints of God. These unregenerate still had the nature of dogs and pigs, though they had cleaned up their appearance. They had, for a season, ceased feeding themselves with their own filthy desires, but God is not mocked, you can't serve two masters. These unsaved *churchgoers* returned fully to the world from which they came, a world they never entirely discarded.

*Second Peter 2:20-22* does not refer to saved Christians, but to those who have played the part. If you know you love the Lord, and you've received him into your life, be at peace concerning your salvation. We live holy to please God our Father. We don't do it to keep from going to hell. Hell is no longer a part of our future. God has written your name in the book of life, and no one will blot it out (Revelation 3:5).

## Risk of falling from Grace

"Knowing that a man is not justified by the works of the law, but by the faith of Jesus Christ, and we have believed in Jesus Christ, that we might be justified by the faith of Christ, and not by the works of the law: for by the works of the law shall no one be justified." – Gal. 2:16

Knowing this, no one shall be justified by the works of the law. No person can be justified by acts of righteousness. We only find justification in having faith in Jesus Christ. Belief in him, belief that brings about acceptance of him as your Lord and Savior, is what God looks for from you in relation to salvation. *Come to Jesus as you are.* Bring all of your issues, faults, and infirmities. Come as you are; God will bring deliverance and help you become the person he desires you to be. God's first desire is that you accept his son, Jesus. Whosoever shall call on the name of Jesus shall be saved! And it's all by his grace. We are no longer under the dispensation of the law, but the dispensation of God's grace.

"I do not frustrate the grace of God: for if righteousness [come] by the law, then Christ is dead in vain." – Gal. 2:21

Many people frustrate the grace of God. He so loved the world that he gave his only begotten son, and whoever believes in him shall not perish, but have everlasting life. God did not send his son into the world to condemn the world, but so the world, through him, might be saved. Jesus came, he died for our sins, and God placed mankind under the dispensation of his grace. We frustrate the grace of God when we complicate the way to salvation.

"For by grace are you saved" the voice of God cries out. Instead of trusting God at his word, we invent additional procedures to assure us of our salvation. We accuse Jesus of not finishing the work he was sent to do. If we must do anything to secure our salvation, then Christ's work on Calvary was incomplete!

"Christ is become of no effect unto you, whosoever of you who are justified by the law; you are fallen from grace." – Gal. 5:4

If we are justified by the law, or justified by works, Jesus' death did nothing for your sins. The stripes he received did nothing for your healing. If you believe you are justified by your good works, all that Christ did is of no benefit to you. You can do nothing to save yourself or secure your salvation. Yes, Paul said to work out your own salvation, but he's not saying that we have to work out the details of securing our salvation. Paul is encouraging us to work out the details of responding to it. We must respond to being saved by putting God first in our lives.

We are saved by grace, and because of that grace, we ought to live a life of gratitude to God who has endowed such grace upon us. We strive to live holy because God is holy. If a child has a good father, that child desires to imitate the behavior and character of that father. God is a good Father, and we, as his children, should strive to imitate him. Because of our love for God, we keep his commandments. And we should always understand that it is because of his mercy that we are not consumed. Someone needs to shout hallelujah!

**You Are Safe and Sealed**

"Not by works of righteousness that we have done, but according to his mercy he saved us, by the washing of regeneration, and renewing of the Holy Ghost." – Tit. 3:5

God is a merciful God; his mercy endures forever, and it is because of God's mercy we aren't consumed. Yet some of us grieve the Holy Spirit on a daily basis. We walk in lust, bitterness, malice, and deception, but God, in his mercy, continues to tolerate our failure to live Christ-like and walk as mature Christians. Many of us walk in the flesh more than the spirit, but God is a long-suffering God. Many of our good deeds, if tested by fire, would burn like straw. If keeping our salvation were up to us, we would certainly lose it. If you believe you can lose your salvation, you *must* also believe (*according to the word)* it is impossible to get it back. According to the scriptures, you would have to crucify Jesus all over again to be saved. But, thank God, our salvation is safe in his hands. It is good to know that when Jesus comes back, he's coming back for you.

In whom you also [trusted], after that you heard the word of truth, the gospel of your salvation: in whom also after that you believed, you were sealed with that Holy Spirit of promise." – Eph 1:13

The word of truth is a phrase used by Jews, referring to a heavenly doctrine. The heavenly doctrine Paul refers to is the gospel of Jesus Christ. After they heard the word of truth (*the gospel of Jesus*), they believed. They believed that Jesus came down from heaven and lived a life free of sin, with which the Father was well pleased. They believed, through the power of God working in Jesus, the sick were healed, the lame walked, the blind received their sight, and the dead were raised. They believed, as we do today, that Jesus died on the cross for our sins, and with his stripes, we were healed. The gospel was preached to us, and we believed. Now comes the test of our faith. The devil will challenge our belief; he will use different situations to cause us to doubt our salvation. If you're not careful, before you know it, doubt will rob you of your assurance of eternal life.

It is a sad thing to fall from grace. Salvation is either by grace *or* by works. You must decide what you believe. If works are, *in any way,* a requirement for salvation, then grace ceases to exist. How can we call salvation a gift if works secure it? If works are needed, salvation *becomes simply compensation for a job well done.*

Once again, in review—Paul said that after we believed, we were sealed with the Holy Spirit of promise. The word "seal" found in this verse comes from the Greek word *sphragizo,* meaning "sealed up for security: from Satan, to confirm, authenticate, and to place beyond doubt."

If you have believed and accepted Christ as your Lord and Savior, you are safe and sealed by that Holy Spirit of promise, and no device made by the devil or man can break that seal. Nothing can remove the seal of the Holy Spirit. In biblical times, a king's seal could not be removed, broken, or tampered with by anyone, except by the king or his order. In another analogy, food is often stored in sealed containers for protection, keeping the food from spoiling. In this same way, we have been sealed—kept by the Holy Spirit until Jesus returns.

"And grieve not the Holy Spirit of God, whereby ye are sealed unto the day of redemption." – Eph. 4:30

Prayerfully, it has been established that we are sealed by the Holy Spirit of promise, and in continuation of this, I want to emphasize again that the sealing is unto the day of redemption, the day that Jesus comes back for his church. The word tells us not to grieve the Holy Spirit. The Holy Spirit was promised and sent to us to teach us all things, and to be our comforter. To grieve the Spirit is to *lupeo* the Spirit, or make him sorry, or cause grief to him.

There are many ways we risk grieving the Holy Spirit. When we tell a lie, cheat, steal, or commit fornication, adultery, or the like, we grieve the Spirit. I would like to reiterate—you can also grieve the Spirit by thinking you are in control of securing your salvation. After the agony of the cross, Jesus exclaimed that it was finished. The redeeming work he came to do was completed. It was finished! Adam sinned in the Garden of Eden, and his sins separated all mankind from God, but God had a plan. (Isn't it great to know that God, even before Adam's sin, had a plan to redeem mankind)?

It was God's plan that Jesus would shed his blood

for the sins of the world. No one else was qualified. Noah wasn't. Noah stumbled after the flood. Abraham wasn't because of his deception in Egypt. Moses wasn't because he failed to give God his glory at the rock. David couldn't; he had too much blood on his hands. Solomon fell short because of his lust for women. God needed a man born of a virgin—a man who would be tempted, as everyone else, yet was without sin.

God needed a man who would turn the other cheek when offended by others, a man who would put the Father's business first. There was no man qualified, so God sent his only begotten son. The Son of God was born of a virgin and walked among us, and we beheld his glory. The glory of the only begotten of the Father, full of grace and truth. His name is Jesus. He turned water into wine, made the blind see, and healed sickness and disease. He even raised the dead. Judas betrayed him, but he knew about the betrayal before it occurred. When they came to take Jesus away, he was ready to go. They railroaded him, and he did not open his mouth. He bore the cross thinking about you and me. They put thorns on his head, mocked him, and led him to the slaughter. Then he got up on the cross and said, "Forgive them Father, 'cause they know not what they do." Your sins, my sins, and the sins of all mankind were placed on him, and he said, "It is finished!" The veil that separated man from God was torn down the middle. It was finished! The redeemer had come and completed the work. Mankind could now be reconciled with his Creator through belief in Jesus. He did it all! All we had to do was receive him.

There's nothing else needed or that can be done to secure your salvation. All we need to do is confess Jesus as our Lord and Savior, believe in our hearts that God raised him from the dead, and we shall be saved. If you believe, and you've already made that confession, I have great news for you—you are *safe* and saved according to the word of God. Don't allow the devil to tell you different. You might not feel saved right now, but salvation is by faith, and it's not by how you feel. If you fall into sin, get up and continue your course. Don't allow the enemy to tempt you into condemnation and self-pity; don't allow the devil to confound you into doubting your salvation. God loves you, and he's not finish with you. You're a diamond in the rough.

# CHAPTER 8

"He that have ears, let him hear what the Spirit says unto the churches; to him that overcomes will I give to eat of the tree of life, which is in the midst of the paradise of God." – Rev. 2:7

"He that has an ear, let him hear what the Spirit says unto the churches; He that overcomes shall not be hurt of the second death." – Rev. 2:11

"He that has an ear, let him hear what the Spirit says unto the churches; To him that overcomes will I give to eat of the hidden manna, and will give him a white stone, and in the stone a new name written, which no man knows except he that receives [it]." – Rev. 2:17

"He that overcomes, the same shall be clothed in white garments; and I will not blot out his name out of the book of life, but I will confess his name before my Father, and before his angels." – Rev. 3:5

"He that overcomes shall inherit all things, and I will be his God, and he shall be my son." – Rev. 21:7

In the preceding verses, promises from God are made to all who overcome. The overcomers shall eat from the tree of life, which is in the midst of the paradise of God. The overcomer shall not be hurt by the second death. The overcomer shall eat of the hidden manna. There shall be a white stone, and in the stone a new name written and given him. The overcomer shall be clothed with white raiment, his name shall not be blotted out of the book of life, and Jesus shall confess his name before the Father and his angels. The overcomer shall inherit all things; God will be his God, and he shall be God's son.

I don't know what you see, but I see many benefits in being an overcomer. The overcomer gets to share in the things of God. You get to eat of the heavenly provisions. God will get personal with you and give you a new name. He will clothe and nurture you. He will be your God forever. I love the benefits of being an overcomer. *But* who are the overcomers, and how do we become an overcomer? Look closely at what an overcomer is. The word overcomer comes from the Greek word *nikaw,* or *nikao,* which means "To conquer, to prevail, to get the victory." Paul wrote by the inspiration of the Holy Spirit when he wrote, "Nay, in all these things we are more than conquerors through him that loved us."

The verses concerning *overcomers* could leave you confused about salvation by grace if you're not rightly diving the word. At first glance, these verses leave one with the impression that salvation is secured by holding on and not giving in. Some scriptures leave one with the impression that works are needed to maintain and secure our salvation, and because of these scriptures, many Christians live in fear of falling short of salvation and missing out on the rapture. Beloved, God has not given us a spirit of fear! We can be certain of our salvation. Now, concerning the verses found in revelation, understand that they were written for the benefit of people under a *different dispensation*. We are presently under the *dispensation of grace*, but during the time of the great tribulation, mankind will be under the *dispensation of judgment*. Under the dispensation of judgment, more works (so to speak) will be required of individuals. After the rapture of the church, faith in Christ and works will be required. Faith and works will be the measuring rod of salvation, for all who are left behind during the tribulation period. Many will have to give their lives for the faith. There will be great martyrdom during this period. Christians will be the target of abuse and cruelty. Many will take the mark of the beast in fear of losing their lives. Christians will have to overcome great persecution to enjoy the promises of God. But, thank God, we are under a *different dispensation*. We are under the *dispensation of grace*. Grace is God's unmerited favor. We did nothing to earn it, and under the dispensation of grace, we become overcomers by faith.

To be an overcomer is to be a conqueror. It is written, "We are more than conquerors through him (Jesus) that loved us." Our status and relationship with Christ has made us more than conquerors. This is accomplished, not by our merits, but through Jesus and his love for us. We are more than conquerors because he is more than a conqueror, and we share in his dominion.

Someone may say, "Pastor Ross, I don't feel like a conqueror *or* overcomer." So what! Walk by faith, not by sight—not by the way you feel or what someone has said about you. "The just shall live by faith." Believe the word of God, you are truly a new person in Christ. Old things have passed away; behold, all things are made new. All things are of God in your life; if you just believe God and allow him to establish you, you will begin to walk as a conqueror.

"For whatsoever is born of God overcomes the world: and this is the victory that overcomes the world, [even] our faith." – 1 John 5:4

If you have truly accepted Jesus as your Lord and Savior, you have been born again. "For as many as received him (Jesus), to them gave he the right to become children of God." We are born of God through receiving the Lord Jesus as our Lord and Savior. Being born of God placed us in the position as an overcomer; it is not by works, but by grace through faith that we are declared overcomers.

**We have heard the voice**

"Who is he that overcomes the world, but he that believes that Jesus is the Son of God?" – 1 John 5:5

An overcomer is one who prevails, and my friends, we have prevailed! We have turned away from the lies of the devil. We've overcome the false doctrines of religions taught throughout this world. We've overcome the evolutionary lie concerning the big bang, and when they couldn't get that lie straight, they tried to make monkeys out of us and wanted us to believe we descended from apes. Then evolutionists came up with fish stories and omnipotent cells, but we overcame all of those lies and held fast to our belief that *in the beginning,* God created. We don't believe in a creation story. We believe in creation facts.

We heard the voice of God, crying in the wilderness of our hearts, saying, "Now is the time for salvation; today is the day." We overcame the doubts so many people are in bondage to—doubts of Jesus' incarnation, the virgin birth, and Jesus' death, burial, and resurrection. And most of all, we overcame doubts of Jesus' deity as the Son of God. "Who is the one that overcomes the world, but he that believes that Jesus is the Son of God, the one that God sent to die for our sins." The question was asked, and answered, "Who is he that overcomes the world? It is all who believes that Jesus is the Son of God." You see, being an overcomer goes back to having faith in the redeeming work of Jesus Christ and who he is.

**The Just shall live by faith**

"He that overcomes, the same shall be clothed in white garments; and I will not blot out his name out of the book of life, but I will confess his name before my Father, and before his angels." - Rev. 3:5

You have been declared an overcomer through your faith in Jesus Christ. When you received him into your life, a decree went forth, declaring you an overcomer. A special order was placed on your behalf for garments of righteousness. The book of life was opened and a note was place by your name that read, *"Never blot this name out."* Then Jesus told God the Father and the angels about you. Jesus will remember you on that special day when the overcomers will be called up, and we will forever be with the Lord. Amen!

**Your salvation was sealed when you accepted Christ as your Lord and Savior!**

You may be asking, "If my salvation is secured by the Holy Spirit, what happens when a Christian sins? Since I don't have to worry about losing my salvation, can I have a sin party and act like the unsaved?" *God forbids!* We can't just live a life of sin without consequences. The Bible tells us, "Who the Lord loves, he chastens." A Christian's sin brings chastisement from God (not damnation). Sin causes us to live a defeated life here on earth. Sin opens the door for sickness, poverty, and spiritual malnutrition. When we sin as Christians, we leave the secret place of the most-high God and step out from under his protective shadow. God wants us to live victorious, healthy, and prosperous lives. Jesus set the stage and was an example, tempted in all points as we are, yet without sin. We can follow Jesus' lead. "Pick up your cross and follow me," says the Lord. We can live Christ-like, because we can do all things through Christ who gives us strength. You *can* have dominion over sinful desires. You *can* walk upright.

You have been bought with a price; therefore, you are free to live a holy and righteous life. No longer do you have to give in to every sinful thought. No longer must you be bound by lustful desires. Now, thanks be to God and our Lord and Savior Jesus Christ, you are free. You're more than a conqueror; therefore, walk in your calling. God has saved you. He paid the price; the work of salvation is complete, and nothing more is needed. The deal is closed, finished, and the specifics have been finalized. The Holy Spirit has you safe and sealed as we wait for Jesus' return.

My friend Mitchell came into my office one day, after months of torment, thinking he'd lost his salvation. He walked in, smiling, and said, "Brother Doug, I got my salvation back." I embraced him with a smile and said, "Brother Mitchell, you never lost your salvation; you simply lost your joy. You never left the Father's hands, but you allowed condemnation to settle in your heart and rob you of your faith in God's grace."

Don't allow the devil to trick you into thinking you're no longer saved because of mistakes you've made. You may not pray as long as my wife Gwen does, but you're still in God's hands. You may not know as many scriptures as Rev. Word does, but you're still in God's hands. And if you've fallen and committed sin, repent and ask God to forgive you. Pick yourself up and continue your Christian walk; press towards the mark of the high calling of God. As the vessel was marred in the potter's hands, you may be marred also. You may not be perfect, but God can still use you. God will never leave or forsake you. Because you're in his hands, God can fix whatever problems you may be having in your Christian walk. If you've left the house of God, come back home. Come back to God. *The Father still loves you.* – Amen!

# The Conclusion

# In Conclusion

It is my prayer that this book has brought relief to your spirit concerning your salvation. You are safe. If you have accepted Jesus Christ as your Lord, then Jesus has a place prepared for you in the Father's house. If you haven't accepted Jesus as your Lord and Savior, you need to do so. Now is the time for salvation; today is the day. Don't put this off. Too many people are dying in their sins. Don't allow the devil to deceive you into thinking you're not ready to live for Christ because of things you are doing. Come to Jesus as you are, and he'll clean you up. He will separate your sins as far as the East is from the West. He will wash you in his blood. He will make all things new in your life. You don't want to leave this world without *having* a relationship with the Lord Jesus Christ. Jesus is the only way you can avoid eternal damnation. If you leave this world without Jesus in your life, you will find out the true meaning of—catching hell.

God has sat before you life and death. His desire is that you choose life. Eternal life is available through Jesus. The word says, "In him is life, and the life is the light of men." Jesus died on the cross that you may have life, and have it more abundantly. Call on the Lord Jesus Christ today. God makes salvation available to all who believe. For he says, "Whoever calls on the name of the Lord Jesus Christ shall be saved." All you need do is repent, turn from the world, and turn to Jesus.

If you confess with your mouth that you desire Jesus to be your Lord and Savior, and you believe in your heart that God raised him from the dead, you shall be saved. For with the heart man believes unto right standing with God, and with the mouth, confession is made unto salvation. The belief in your heart stands against all doubt. Your belief is pleasing to God because it represents your faith, and without faith, it is impossible to please God. The confession with your mouth is equally important; out of the abundance of the heart, a man speaks. We are made aware by the word of God that life and death reside in the power of what we say. The word "confession" comes from the Greek word *omologew*, which is defined as "profess, promise, acknowledge, to concede, to declare, and to say the same thing as another, i.e. to agree with, assent." These words beautifully define confession, but I want to elevate the word "concede." To confess or concede to the Lord Jesus is conceding to who he is, what he has done, and what he will do. When you confess with your mouth the Lord Jesus, you are saying that Jesus is Lord of Lords, and most importantly, you have conceded to him being your Lord. God has given us these instructions as a way for us to receive the gift of salvation. I pray you will call on and accept Jesus into your life today, that you may know the love of God and discover his grace.

## Prayer for Salvation

God sent his only son, Jesus, to die for you, and on the third day, God raised him from the dead. If you haven't received Christ into your life, and you would like to do so, simply pray this prayer:

> *Lord Jesus*—I now turn from the world, and I turn to you. I believe God sent you into the world to save sinners, and I confess that I am a sinner. I believe you died for my sins, and God raised you from the dead. And I believe you are alive forever more.
>
> *Lord Jesus*—I confess and believe that you are Lord of Lords, and I ask that you come into my life and become my Lord and Savior.
>
> Lord Jesus—may you live and reign in me, and allow me to live in you. Jesus, wash me from all unrighteousness and fill me with your holy spirit.
>
> In Jesus' name, I pray—Amen!

# Poems

By Gwendolyn Ross

## Thank You, Father

I want to thank you, Father,
for saving my life.
From so much heartache,
and so much strife.
I want to thank you, Father,
for giving me peace;
*Now I know the madness has completely ceased.*

I want to thank you, Father,
for giving me grace;
Without fear of losing, I can run this Christian race.
I want to thank you, Father,
for giving me power;
*Now I can defeat the devil at any tempting hour.*

I want to thank you, Father,
for all that you've done.
You love me so much
*you gave*
your only begotten Son.

## I'm on My Way

I command you to stop sinning and doing your own thing
Before you feel my wrath, and my powerful sting.
I command you to line up with my word today,
To stop the death and destruction that is on its way.
I command you to walk in righteousness, truth, and to put away guile.
So you can preach the gospel to everyone.
Man,
    woman,
        and
            child.
For I've given you power to make the devil flee,
So you can walk and run, in total victory.
So get your house in order; I'm on my way.
For no one knows the hour, the time, or the day!

# Resources
# Products Listing
by Pastor Douglas L. Ross

## Audio and Video Products

Pastor Douglas L. Ross

| Resource for Christian Conduct and Personal Development | |
|---|---|
| **Cassette Tapes $5.00 ea.** | |
| C06P | Living with Purpose |
| C08P | Pressure |
| C09P | 6 Ways to Please God |
| C20P | Our God is an Awesome God |
| C26P | The Ministry in You |
| C29P | I Can Change |
| C33P | A Need for Patience |
| C34P | Trust in God |
| C39P | Integrity |
| C42P | Have You Seen Jesus? |
| C43P | The Next Level |
| C52P | Tight with God |
| C56P | Submit to Authority |
| C59P | Forgiveness |
| C61P | Knowledge of God |
| C74P | The Prodigal Son 2 (A Question of Love) |
| C75P | Let Your Light Shine |
| C79P | Recognizing the Voice of God |
| C98P | How to Operate on the Next Level |
| C100P | A Spirit of Excellence |

| | |
|---|---|
| C107P | Operating in Excellence with Consistency |
| C109P | How to Forget about the Past and m Move Forward |

## Prayer and Praise

| | |
|---|---|
| C16P | Undignified Praise |
| C44P | Jesus is the One |

## Faith

| | |
|---|---|
| C08P | Thank You Faith |
| C54P | F.A.I.T.H. Is |
| C65P | Look and Live |
| C68P | If God Be for You |
| C113P | You Got Power! |
| C112P | How Far Will You Go? |

## Deliverance

| | |
|---|---|
| C05P | I'm Coming Out |
| C19P | I Can Change |
| C23P | Stop Lying |
| C62p | Murmuring and Complaining |
| C96P | Deliverance |

## Prosperity

| | |
|---|---|
| C55P | The Power of the Seed |
| C57P | Water the Seed |
| C80P | Jabez (More Honorable) |
| C88P | P & C - The Road to Success |
| C115P | The Day Has Come |

## Salvation & Healing

| | |
|---|---|
| C02P | Life Insurance |

## Resource for Church Order and Ministry

| | |
|---|---|
| C04P | Democracy - Not in God's House |
| C38P | Order in the House |
| C49P | High Treason |
| C58P | Help Your Church Grow |
| C78P | Defining the Role of an Elder |
| C109P | Understanding Your Call to Ministry |
| C110P | Fulfilling Your Call to Ministry |
| C82P | A Place to Belong |

## Holiday Messages

| | |
|---|---|
| C03P | The Real Christmas Story |
| C37P | Triumphant Entry |

## VHS Video Tapes

VHS Tapes $10.00

| | |
|---|---|
| V04P | The Ministry in You |
| V06P | Living with Purpose |
| V07P | Good Advice, Bad Advice |
| V08P | Come Clean |
| V09P | An Ordinary Person |
| V11P | 6 Ways to Please God |
| V12P | Friends Winning Friends |

## Other Books by Douglas L. Ross:

**Blue Book of Faith Confession**
ISBN: 978-0-9796-0770-7
Page: 148
Price: $10.95 *U.S.*

For additional copies of

*I'm Still in His Hands*

And to order tapes from the product listing, please write:

DGR Christian Books
P.O. Box 9333
Richmond, Virginia 23227

*or visit us at:*

**God Chasers International Church**
**4700 N. Southside Plaza Drive**
**Richmond, Virginia 23224**

*or call:* 804 230-6548

*Order online at:*
DGRchristianbooks.com
www.gchasers.com

www.ingramcontent.com/pod-product-compliance
Lightning Source LLC
LaVergne TN
LVHW050934080826
845145LV00004B/1251

* 9 7 8 0 9 7 9 6 0 7 7 1 4 *